W9-CED-878

CASTLES

CASTLES

BETH SMITH

Illustrations by Anne Canevari Green

Franklin Watts
New York / London / Toronto / Sydney / 1988

A First Book

*The castle that appears on page 10 is
Chenonceaux Castle, located in the Loire Valley, France.*

Cover photograph by J. Gordon Miller, Shostal Associates.

Photographs courtesy of: Art Resource: pp. 10 (SEF), 14, 32 (Giraudon), 36,
42 (bottom), 57, 59 (Giraudon), 61 Alinari; Photo Researchers, Inc.: pp. 13
(Fritz Henle), 19 (Tia Schneider Denenberg), 39 (bottom—George Whiteley),
42 (top—Georg Gerster); Peter Menzel: pp. 16, 29 (bottom), 64, 71, 77;
The British Tourist Authority: p. 26; The Bettmann Archive, Inc.: pp. 29 (top),
39 (top), 45, 49, 52 (both), 68, 73, 76; Swiss National Tourist Office: p. 79.

Library of Congress Cataloging-in-Publication Data

Smith, Beth.
Castles / Beth Smith; [illustrations by Anne Canevari Green].
p.   cm. — (A First book)
Bibliography: p.
Includes index.
Summary: Discusses the design and use of European castles from 500
A.D., relates what daily life was like inside, and presents legends
and ghost stories linked with castles.
ISBN 0-531-10511-3
1. Castles—Juvenile literature.   2. Civilization, Medieval—
Juvenile literature.   [1. Castles.   2. Civilization, Medieval.
3. Castles—Folklore.]   I. Green, Anne Canevari, ill.   II. Title.
CC135.S55   1988
940.1—dc19   87-25181   CIP   AC

6

CONTENTS

For Dad,
who always had the time

CASTLES

ONE

WHAT IS
A CASTLE?

When castles were built hundreds of years ago, they had two basic purposes. First, they provided shelter and living space for those within. Second, and more importantly, they were designed to keep people out, to refuse entry to a group of people—the enemy. Today, churches, stores, and houses usually have locks on the doors to keep people from entering at certain times. But a lock on the door would not have stopped an army from invading a castle. For similar reasons, protecting those who lived within one of these buildings took precedence over all other housing requirements. By surrounding themselves with strong walls, people inside the castle felt safe and were free to do as they wished without fear. They had created a stronghold that was much better than a locked door. Safety was very important, and comfort in the earliest castles was a minor consideration.

The word *castle* evolved over many centuries from the Latin word *castrum*, meaning a closed fort or stronghold. By the tenth century A.D. there was a Latin word, *castellum*, which meant a fortified house of a landowner. Gradually, this became the accepted meaning of *castellum* in a number of European languages. The words castle, *chateau, kastil,* and *castello* all signify a dwelling meant for both living purposes and defense.

The number of castles in Europe shows how widespread the need for defense was during the Middle Ages, or from about A.D. 500 to 1400. Castles were also a sign of power and success. Kings and rulers desired them, but so did landowners who wanted to show their wealth and power in the regions where they lived. Because of this, there were basically two kinds of castles: royal and baronial.

Royal castles belonged to the king. He would build castles for political reasons such as demonstrating the strength of the crown's authority. Sometimes, although rarely, castles served as a means of terrorizing nearby towns or villages. Or the king built castles to defend important places both on the edge of his kingdom and within it. These strategic locations in the interior of a kingdom might include major transportation routes such as passes, fords, or narrow valleys.

A baronial castle belonged to a lord or baron of a certain designated area, which was called a fief. A fief was land not privately owned, but rather taken care of by a lord or vassal for another greater lord, in exchange for military service. From the ninth to the fifteenth century, a feudal system existed in Europe. Because of the feudal system a great many

Blenheim Castle, in England, is an example of a baronial castle.

castles were built. The baron would position his castle in the best place to defend his own territory from others. Usually each baron protected his own property; however, in some areas, a few baronial castle owners teamed together to support each other. Some of the early baronial castles were on sites selected because they were difficult to reach, because of swamps, marshes, ditches, cliffs, or man-made lakes. This was a way of defending the castle from the enemy.

If a private or baronial castle occupied a place in the interior, a king would usually try to gain control of it. Some castles in strategic locations were built at mountain passes high in the Alps. Tolls were collected at these castles from those who used the passes. At other castles, such as those along the Rhine Valley in Germany, tolls were collected from merchants who used the river for transportation.

Castles were built to be defensive, yet they had offensive capabilities, too. The offensive strength of the castle came from the soldiers it housed. A castle offered a safe military base for both mounted and unmounted soldiers.

Some castles were never under siege and never received a scratch. Others were constantly attacked, and some were even destroyed in battle. Some castles served only as administration centers of a kingdom; others were built to be strong military bases. Some were buildings of great beauty and luxury while others were bleak and cold and hardly more than a cave.

An illustration depicting
the feudal system

*Alcazar Castle is located high above the town
of Segovia, Spain, for easier defense.*

Thousands of castles were built during medieval times. In Germany alone, over 10,000 were reportedly constructed. The building of castles was widespread. They can be found in countries such as Italy, Switzerland, Portugal, Sicily, France, Great Britain, Russia, Denmark, Poland, Syria, Turkey, Jordan, and many more. Spain alone has more than 2,500 in existence. Poland has 450, and Belgium over 900. Some of the many castles still standing are lived in and are enjoyed as spacious homes.

But to understand castles and what they meant, we have to look at them from the perspective of when they were built. Historians now see castles as the most enduring, important element in medieval society, the peak of the Middle Ages.

TWO

EARLY CASTLES

As early as the 800s A.D., castles existed in France. Many of the early castles were constructed in order to defend against invasions. The Vikings attacked the shores of Britain and northern Europe. The Hungarians, coming from the east, pressed into present-day France and Germany. The Saracens, sailing from northern Arabia, raided Italy, Sicily, and Spain. Sweden had a number of castles to protect itself from pirates on its eastern shore. The early German castles were tall wooden towers called *bergfrieden*.

In 1066, just after England had successfully defeated an invading Viking force, William the Conqueror and his Norman forces fought England. Weary and weakened, the English were unprepared for battle and had few castles and fortifications that could withstand an invasion. Victorious, William the Conqueror crowned himself King of England in October of 1066.

William the Conqueror was a Norman. Normandy was a region of what is now France, and the Normans were skilled castle builders. Necessity had taught them to build strong

This castle was built by William the Conqueror in Normandy, France, during the eleventh century. From this castle, he set out on his conquest of England. It has been restored in stone to preserve it.

castles after being invaded by other countries and having had a number of civil wars.

Upon arriving in England, William the Conqueror began building castles. Most of them weren't the usual stone castles that we think of today, but wooden ones called motte-and-bailey castles. He built one of these in many of the towns he occupied. Most were built within a few months or weeks. Over 90 percent of the original castles built by William the Conqueror were motte-and-bailey castles. In the years 1066 to 1100 about five hundred of these castles were built in England. Over one hundred of them guarded all roads into London from within a radius of 60 miles (96 km).

The motte was a mound of earth 10 to 100 feet (3.5-35 m) high. If possible, a natural hill or mound was used for the motte. If the terrain of an area was flat, a motte was built up by heaping a huge mound of earth and then packing it down. The motte was usually built first. Then soldiers on sentry duty could warn the workers of any impending danger approaching the castle.

Around the top of the motte was a wooden fence or palisade 10 or 12 feet (3.5–4 m) high. There was a sentry walk built along the inside of the palisade so that the surrounding countryside could be viewed at all times. Inside the palisade was a wooden tower. Sometimes the tower was brightly colored and ornately carved and decorated. Some towers stood on wooden pillars with a bridge or stairs to the first floor. Others were built with the first floor at ground level. The wooden tower of the motte varied in size from a small, narrow one-room tower to a large tower with many rooms and more than one floor. Around the motte there was a moat or wide, deep ditch for added protection. Often the moat was filled with water, but sometimes it was left dry.

There was some variety in the way motte-and-bailey castles were constructed. In Hertfordshire, England, one was excavated that originally had a 60-foot (18-m) -high tower on the motte with an entryway through a tunnel lined with timber.

The bailey was an oval or sometimes rectangular area on the level ground below the motte. If the bailey was oval shaped, the motte and bailey together would make the shape of a figure eight. The bailey would also have a palisade and a moat or ditch around its perimeter. There was a gate at the farthest point from the motte. If invaders were to break through the bailey gate, they were still some distance from the tower in the motte. If there was an attack, the bailey might be evacuated, and defenders would withdraw onto the motte.

The bailey gave protection to the local peasants and their farm animals during times of siege. The peasants who helped build the castle also were often expected to help defend it in emergencies. The baron or landowner expected help from the peasants, but in return he would protect them from outside dangers.

The bailey varied in size from as small as 1 acre (.40 ha) to as large as 6 or 7 acres (2.5 or 3 ha) if there was a natural defensible outline such as a coastline, cliff, or a sheer stone wall that made fortifying the bailey easier.

There was also another early castle very similar to the motte-and-bailey castle called the ring-motte castle. It was a variation in which the motte was not raised, but was protected by very steep banks of earth that had been dug out from a ditch that encircled the motte.

Within the bailey were many of the necessities of a castle. There was a kitchen or cookhouse which was far enough

Motte-and-Bailey Castle

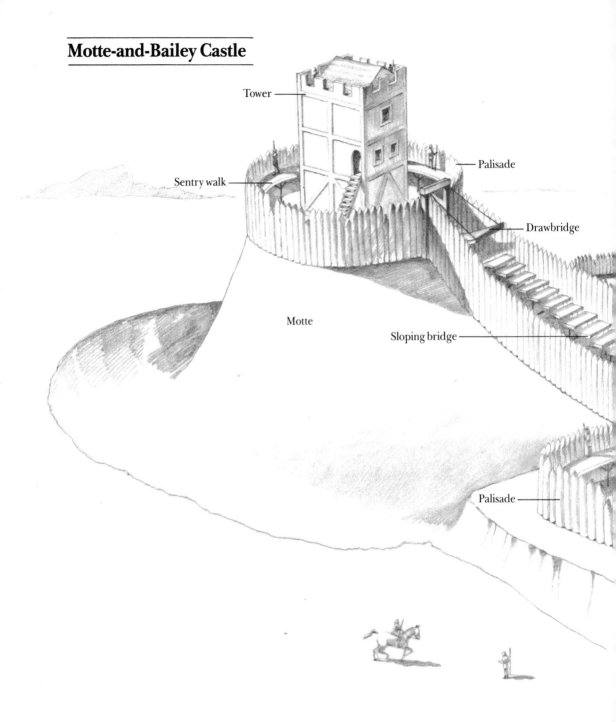

Tower

Palisade

Sentry walk

Drawbridge

Motte

Sloping bridge

Palisade

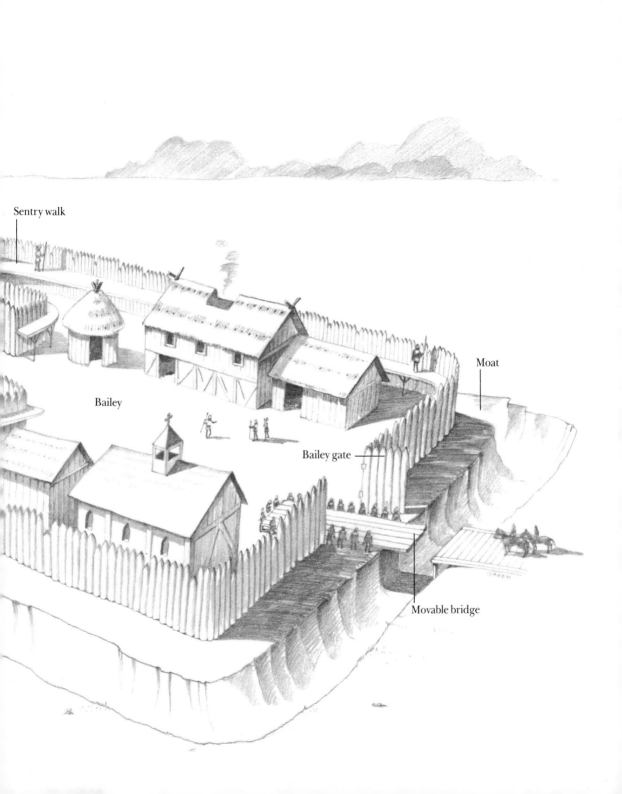

Sentry walk

Bailey

Bailey gate

Moat

Movable bridge

from the motte so that the cooking fire could not set the wooden tower on fire. There was a wooden hall for common meals. There were also bakehouses, brewhouses, barns or pens for the cattle and horses, storehouses, attendants' living quarters, usually a chapel, and workshops and huts for the skilled craftsmen. These buildings often were built with thatched roofs. In some motte-and-bailey castles, the tower on the motte also had a thatched roof.

Access to the motte from the bailey was via a sloping bridge that sometimes had a drawbridge on the motte end. Entrance to the motte could then be barred if the enemy overran the bailey. Some mottes had a gatehouse; others had only a platform over the gate from which soldiers could defend it.

Since motte-and-bailey castles could be constructed in a few weeks and didn't require many skilled craftsmen, a lord or baron could use local peasant labor and sometimes build the entire castle before a ruler or king would know about it. When William the Conqueror won the Battle of Hastings in 1066, he put together a motte-and-bailey castle in one day by bringing precut timbers from on board his ships.

If the wooden towers or palisades were ruined in a siege, they could be rebuilt fairly quickly. There is a story of a motte-and-bailey castle built in 1139 by the Frenchman Henry of Beaubourg that was erected literally overnight. He was at war with Arnold of Ardres, and he had a wooden castle pre-fabricated secretly and moved to the site of a destroyed castle during the middle of the night. The next morning, Arnold and his troops were faced with a finished wooden castle that they finally did overtake, but only with great effort.

From what we know today, early castles were not very

luxurious. In the tower on the motte there may have been only one large room where the lord and his household ate, lived, and slept. The lord would receive guests and carry on business in this room during the day. The meals would be served there. Then at night the tables were moved to one side and straw mats were placed on the floor for sleeping. The lord and his lady might have had their sleeping section separate from the others and curtained off behind the dais. The dais was a raised platform where the lord sat and received people during the day. Castle living was very public. There was little opportunity for privacy.

The roomiest and most luxurious motte-and-bailey castle might have had cellars for storage and a granary on the first floor. The second floor would have been the common living quarters for the workers, and there might have been a separate lord's chamber, and a private room for the children and waiting maids. There also could have been a private room with a fire that was used for heat in the evening or for those who were ill. The third floor was usually the top floor. It would have included a chapel and servants' sleeping areas. Stairs connected all the floors. But this would have been a rather elegant early castle, and an exception to most others.

Stone was expensive and the labor required to build a stone castle was costly. Also, stone construction required a great deal more time. Timber was readily available, making wooden motte-and-bailey castles the better choice.

One very early castle was Cadbury Castle in Great Britain, which was occupied during A.D. 470–500. This was the time when the legendary King Arthur is said to have lived, and some people think that Cadbury Castle might have been his. It consisted of a wooden hall built on top of four level

banks that rose like concentric rings one on top of the other. The top bank was surrounded by a stone and wooden wall for added protection.

The Bayeux Tapestry, an eleventh- or twelfth-century wall hanging that is 231 feet (70 m) long, depicts many scenes of the Norman Conquest of England. It shows William the Conqueror's camp being built and there is an excellent example of a motte-and-bailey castle.

There are no motte-and-bailey castles remaining today, but in many countries the rounded hill of the motte and even the outline of the bailey still can be detected through overgrown brambles and bushes. Some timber castles were later rebuilt as stone castles, keeping the original outline of the motte and bailey. However, most motte-and-bailey castles fell into disuse or were abandoned as timbers rotted, and more spacious and comfortable stone castles were built. Although easily constructed and rather crude, the design of the motte-and-bailey castle was actually advanced for this period in history. These castles served their purpose as strongholds that could control territories that had already been gained and as outposts for further conquests.

The remains of Dundrum Castle,
a motte-and-bailey castle,
in Northern Ireland

THREE

THE FIRST
STONE CASTLES

Wood was cheap, but it was not durable over a long period of time, and could not withstand fire. As a result, stone gradually became the more desirable building material for castles. Stone castles first existed in France as early as the ninth century, while some timber castles remained in use as late as the 1300s. In some countries, such as Holland, where there was a lack of good building stone, more castles were built with brick. One of the most famous Dutch brick castles was Muiderslot built in the 1200s.

In the early twelfth century, the wooden wall on top of the motte was sometimes replaced by a stone wall that was known as a shell keep. Arundel Castle, the early Windsor Castle, and Restormel Castle in England all had shell keeps.

Some of the first stone castles were "revisions" of early timber castles. Square stone keeps replaced the wooden towers on mottes. Keeps were wide, towerlike buildings. At Cardiff Castle in Wales the original motte is still intact with a stone keep that was built in the twelfth century.

Above: *Cardiff Castle,
Wales, with its original
motte. The main part of
the castle is now a school
for music and drama.*
Left: *Parador del Marqués
de Villena, a castle in
Alarcon, Spain. Today,
this castle, like other
paradors in Spain, is a
government-operated hotel.*

Keeps received their name because a king and his men lived there or were "kept" there. Square or rectangular stone keeps could be built higher than the old wooden towers. They were easier to defend and fewer soldiers were needed. Sometimes they stood alone in the inner ward (also known as inner bailey or inner court); others were inserted into the stone wall, which was called a curtain. The stone walls ranged from 12 to 20 feet (4 to 6 m) thick and could withstand most medieval siege artillery except the bore and battering ram. Castle Hedingham and Castle Rising in England and Falaise Castle in Normandy, France all have rectangular keeps and were built in the twelfth century.

In England stone castles were introduced later than on the continent of Europe. Chepstow Castle in Wales was the first stone castle built in Britain. It was finished in A.D. 1071 by William FitzOsbern, a friend and boyhood companion of William the Conqueror. Part of the original castle still stands today.

Some stone castles were built where there had been no earlier wooden castles. It was important to place a castle where it would be safe and where the most damage could be done to an advancing enemy. German castles, like the Boosenburg and the Bromserburg, were usually either high on a mountain or on the banks of a river. In the Middle East, the Crusader castles at Sahyun (or Saône) and Crac (or Krak) des Chevaliers, citadels of the knights in Syria, were built on a three-sided cliff with only one access route that had to be protected with a wall or ditch. That way all defensive efforts could be concentrated on the gate on that one side. Other castles that stood on rocky peaks were those in Lastours and Gaillard, France; Loarre, Spain; and Chepstow, Wales.

The White Tower in the center of the Tower of London

Stone Castle

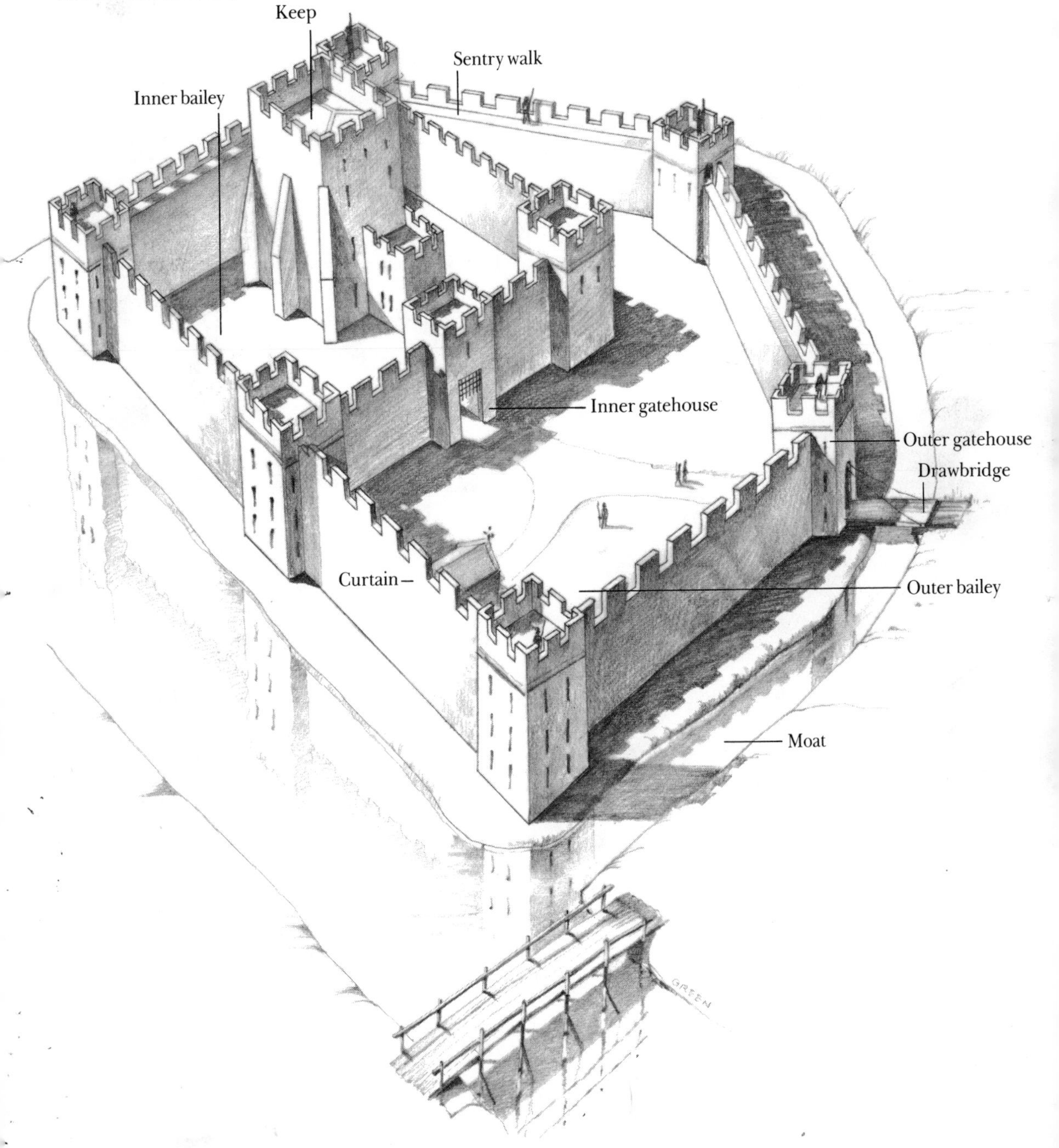

Keep

Sentry walk

Inner bailey

Inner gatehouse

Outer gatehouse

Drawbridge

Curtain

Outer bailey

Moat

GREEN

Crac (Krak) des Chevaliers, Syria

was one of the very first stone keeps designed by William the Conqueror. He also built one at Colchester, England. Both were exceptionally well built and were the equals of keeps built many years later.

The White Tower was built between A.D. 1066 and 1100. It has been altered little even to this day. The keep is 90 feet (27 m) high and has three floors. Each floor was built with two rooms divided by a wall that runs from the top to the bottom of the building. A narrow winding stairway was built in one corner, and in William's day there were two entries into the keep.

The main gate was on the first floor and was large enough for horses to go through. There was also a small door known as a postern on the same level, large enough for men but not horses. Wooden ramps led to these doors that could be removed during a siege. One problem with the two doors was that they were in plain view. If the castle was under attack, it was almost impossible for castle defenders to rush out and surprise the enemy.

The kitchen was also on the first floor. The second floor held the chapel and the great hall where most daily events took place. The third floor included the council chambers and the king's apartment. In the White Tower there was more privacy than in the earlier motte-and-bailey castles, but still everyone lived in close quarters.

The square stone keeps were the strongest kind of castles for about one hundred years until they were finally tested in battle. By then siege tactics had improved, and some weaknesses in their design became apparent. Square or rectangular keeps were weak at the angles or corners, which could be defended only from directly above. Also they were not designed for protection against an enemy who had worked his way to the foot of the outside wall.

The White Tower was a perfect example of this. Inside, the inhabitants were secure behind walls that were 15 feet (4.5 m) thick. But those inside could not strike out easily at the enemy. The windows and arrow slits were narrow so that archers could shoot straight ahead but could not shoot at angles. The square corners of the keep created "blind spots." Archers in the keep could not see out to the corners of the keep. The enemy could hack away in the "blind spot" with picks until they could loosen enough stone to make a hole or make the corner of the keep crumble. Then they could climb over the rubble to attack.

Therefore the design of the keep changed as new ones were built. The curtain or stone wall surrounding the keep was built with a sentry walk along the inside top for archers and crossbowmen. Archers could patrol the wall and have a better range of fire in protecting the keep. It was still difficult, however, for archers or bowmen to shoot at an enemy at the foot of the wall directly below unless they leaned out over the edge. Unfortunately, this made *them* excellent targets.

Knights fighting in difficult places saw many designs and styles of castle building. They eagerly brought back new ideas to their own homelands about the castles they had seen. As a result, building ideas and styles moved from country to country.

After the Crusades to the Holy Land, rulers and knights returned to Europe suggesting that towers be built in the curtain of the castle. This was a major change in castle design. Square or round towers were then constructed that protruded beyond the curtain half the tower's width. These towers were placed at intervals along the curtain and at the corners. They were a story or so higher than the wall itself. Archers could then fire on those below and outside the curtain through windows in the towers. The only stairs to the top of the curtain were in the tower. There was a strong door on the tower leading out to the sentry walk, so that if an enemy reached the top of the wall he could not gain entry to the rest of the castle and could easily be picked off by the archers in the tower.

Eventually, as castle building continued to improve, the top of the castle curtain was crenellated. There were gaps called crenels, and walls between the gaps called merlons. This gave the top of the wall a "toothed" look. Hoards were built as another improvement, and were first used in France. A hoard is a wooden platform that projects out from the upper wall along the sentry walk. To get to the hoards, soldiers would step through the crenels or gaps. The hoards would be directly over the enemy who might reach the wall. The hoards were enclosed to protect soldiers inside and gave them better access to the enemy without exposing themselves as targets. There were holes in the hoards so that hot water, liquid tar, or molten metal could be poured on the enemy.

Over the years it became necessary to strengthen baileys on castles that still had them. At some castles, another bailey was added on lower slopes to protect the townspeople if they were under attack. They could also retreat to the inner walls if the outer walls were overrun.

Square towers eventually gave way to round ones that were not so easy for the enemy to attack. Round towers were more difficult to build, but were worth the effort. Square towers, like the square corners of the keep itself, could crum-

ble when enough stones were hacked from a corner. The field of fire was also improved with the use of the round tower.

Towns existed prior to and independently of castles. However, towns sometimes needed protection as much as those living within a castle. As a direct extension of the castle, a wall might be built around an adjacent town. This wall usually had towers at regular intervals and also towers protecting the gates.

A castle, La Rocca Scaligera, in northern Italy, built in the thirteenth century. Note the crenellated castle curtain.

FOUR

THE CONCENTRIC CASTLE

When round towers were built along the curtain wall, they made strongholds within themselves. By the end of the thirteenth century, the earlier wooden hoards were built of stone as an actual part of the castle wall. With these two improvements the curtain was strong and defenders had a superior range of fire. They could attack an enemy directly below the wall.

The square keep was becoming less popular. There was no longer a need for a stone keep because the curtain could be defended. Rather than a keep, buildings were constructed along the inside of the curtain, and some rooms were built within the walls of the curtain itself. Builders, by this time, could turn their attention to another part of the castle with a potential weakness—the entrance. A strong gatehouse became the most important part of a castle's structure.

At first, the gatehouse had two D-shaped towers with the straight wall facing inward, but later they were circular or octagonal (having eight sides), with the gate recessed

Two different styles of gatehouses. The gatehouse in the drawing is to a French castle. The gatehouse in the photograph is to Lullingstone Castle, Kent, England. It was built around 1497 and is the earliest brick gatehouse in England.

between them. The towers on either side of the gate were two or three stories high with rooms above the gatehouse.

Some castles had a barbican in front of the gatehouse. A barbican was a stone building that stood in front of the gatehouse and led to the gate with adjoining stone walls that narrowed the approach an outsider could make. This prevented a large mass of soldiers from rushing the gatehouse. A sentry was also posted in the barbican.

The portcullis was a crucial part of the gatehouse. It was a heavy door made of wood grating and usually covered with iron. It hung on chains and slid up and down vertical grooves in the gatehouse walls. The lower points of the portcullis were like a row of metal spears. The portcullis was controlled by a winch, a pulley-like mechanism which raised and lowered the portcullis. In an emergency, the portcullis could be dropped at a moment's notice by cutting the rope with an ax.

Often there would be two portcullises: one on the outside of the castle wall, the other on the inner side of the wall ten or fifteen feet away. If the enemy advanced into the gatehouse, both portcullises could be dropped, trapping the intruders between them.

The gatehouse had "murder holes" in the level above the two portcullises. If the enemy were trapped inside, arrows could be shot and boiling liquids could be poured down through these murder holes. On both sides of the portcullis there were slits in the towers so that arrows could also be fired into the contained area from an angle level with it. In this way, the two portcullises helped to create a bold, awe-inspiring entrance.

Toward the end of the thirteenth century, highly developed concentric castles were built in France, England, and

Wales. These were the most advanced examples of medieval architecture that existed. A concentric castle was like two castles in one because there was one set of walls inside another, each one being a complete entity in itself.

Concentric castles were designed so that the inner wall was the higher of the two. In that way castle defenders on the inner wall or curtain had a free range of fire over the heads of those on the outer curtain. Because of the advances that had been made in building towers along a curtain, the defending soldiers in a concentric castle were free to move all around the sentry walks and fire from anywhere.

The area inside the walls of a castle is the ward, or bailey, which means the protected or defended area, also known as courtyard. Bailey can also mean the walls surrounding the ward. In a concentric castle, there was an inner ward within the inner walls, and an outer ward between the inside and the outside walls. The inner ward became the stronghold as the keep was the stronghold in earlier castles.

Cilgerran Castle in Wales was a concentric castle built in the 1200s that was erected on an old motte-and-bailey site. The inner ward was placed on the site of the motte, and the outer ward was built where the bailey had been.

Kidwelly Castle, also in Wales, was a concentric castle that had great natural strength because of its location. The curtain of the outer ward had to be only a semicircle because part of the inner ward stood on the edge of a deep ravine.

The walls of a concentric castle ranged from 12 to 20 feet (4 to 6 m) thick. Walls were often built with good facing stone on either side while the middle would be filled with rubble and mortar. This was cheaper than building solid stone walls. These walls could withstand most artillery of the Middle Ages.

The entrance to the inner ward was between the corner towers and was guarded by a huge, elaborate gatehouse. The outer wall surrounded this and could be as close as only a few yards away. The outer wall would also have towers, stout walls, and a strong gatehouse.

The towers of the castle were not built just for the defense of the castle. Each round tower had three rooms, one above the other. A spiral staircase built into the outside wall joined the floors. The basement or ground floor of the tower was for storage while the first floor was either working space or living area. The first and second floors above the basement were made of wood. The dungeon was below the basement and could be reached only through a trap door in the basement floor. A castle that didn't have a dungeon might use the storerooms on the basement floor for holding a prisoner by simply chaining him to the barrels. The chapel if located in a tower had only one floor above the basement so that it could have a high arching ceiling. Rooms were also built in the upper floors of the gatehouses and within the thickness of the curtain. The variety of rooms in concentric

Above: *an aerial view of Castillo de Bellver, a concentric castle on Mallorca, a Spanish island.* Below: *the walls of a concentric castle, Carcassonne, located in southern France. The inside walls are noticeably higher than the outside walls.*

castles provided much of the privacy that earlier castles lacked.

The inner ward was constructed once the outer ward was made secure with a strong gatehouse. Within the inner ward were more buildings. These were constructed using the inner curtain as one wall and by building the other three sides and floors of timber with a slate roof. Storage areas were on the basement or ground-level floor. The first floor of the same building contained sleeping quarters.

The great hall where the ruler carried on his business was in the inner ward. So was the kitchen, which contained ovens for baking bread, huge fireplaces for smoking and cooking meat, and a storage area for drinks such as wine and ale. Water was piped to a stone sink from a stone cistern or holding tank above the kitchen in a tower. The well was within the inner ward so that it was protected from enemies who might want to poison it.

Some castles also had guest quarters and private quarters for part of the castle staff built in the inner ward. There would also be an area which contained cages for the king's or lord's hunting birds and kennels for his dogs in the inner ward.

Building a concentric castle was a slow process. Some took only five years to build—a relatively short period of time, but some were known to take much longer. Caernarvon in Wales was started in 1283. It took over twenty-five

Caernarvon Castle
in Wales

years to build and was never completely finished as originally planned. Caerphilly Castle in Wales was one of the largest castles in Great Britain. It covered 30 acres (12.1 ha).

A construction crew for a concentric castle could include anywhere from fifteen hundred to three thousand workers. This was a large building force in proportion to the population of a country at that time. They came from long distances and sometimes a guard would be provided for them when traveling through hostile areas. Master masons, for the most part, tended to be well educated, intelligent, and well traveled, and produced highly sophisticated work. But most laborers were unskilled and uneducated. There would also be a resident clerk of works to oversee the labor and handle the financial end of the construction.

Castles were often built on solid rock, in which case stone from the site itself was used in the building. A good deal of stone could be used from the ditches for the moats. Timber for floors, roof, and scaffolding might come from the local area if a forest was nearby. Local sand was used for mortar. More sophisticated work like fireplaces and window casings usually came from special stone transported to the castle. The roof of the castle was constructed from sheets of lead. Lead and iron were also transported, often from great distances.

The building season ran from late spring through fall. Then, during the winter, the unfinished walls were covered with thatch or turf to protect them from the frost until the following spring when construction work would resume.

King Edward I of England built many concentric castles. He was so intrigued by castles that he had an elaborate wooden toy castle made for his son, who was born in Caernarvon Castle. The toy castle was made for the young Prince Edward when he was six by a member of the castle staff.

The military architect who designed King Edward's new castles was Master James of St. George. He was a talented master builder, and was so valuable to the king that he was awarded a life pension.

Some of the most advanced concentric castles were built near the sea so they could be supplied by water. This was safer than crossing unfriendly land for food or reinforcements. Rhuddlan, Beaumaris, and Harlech in Wales, all built in the 1200s, are examples of concentric castles built near the sea that still exist today.

FIVE

DEFENDING A CASTLE

There were many ways of gaining control of a castle. Sometimes these methods were used in combination. In one method, attackers hoped that by knocking down some part of the structure, they would cause those inside to surrender. This artillery barrage was a popular method, but it caused damage to the castle.

Another method was to take a castle by surprise. This was the most difficult method, but it left the castle in perfect condition. When a castle was not at war, there was only a small group of men left there to defend it, making a surprise attack easier. The Scots took Edinburgh Castle from the English in 1341, at a time when the English held the castle. The Scots hid soldiers in a wagonload of hay. The wagon stopped in the gateway, blocking the gate and keeping it open until other soldiers waiting outside the castle came to their aid. Sometimes the inhabitants of the castle were bribed in order to allow the attackers to enter the castle secretly.

Soldiers fighting during a siege

A third method of gaining control of a castle was by siege or blockade. This took longer but was successful if the enemy had the patience to sit it out. In time, those inside the castle would starve, or their wells would run dry. There was also the possible danger that the enemy might poison the well if they could gain access to it. Some castles were able to keep as much as a year's supply of food, but the water supply was more vulnerable. Blockading a castle also involved danger for the attackers as well. A long wait often prompted disease from unsanitary camp conditions, and there was always the possibility that an army might arrive to defend the castle.

One castle was cut off from supplies for three months. Finally the well went dry, and those inside were forced to use wine for all their liquid needs. The castle dwellers had to make bread with wine, boil their food in it, and even use it to douse fires from torches and burning missiles that had been thrown over the castle walls. It didn't take long to use up their supply, and there was little choice but to surrender.

Most castles could not hold back an enemy indefinitely, but were built with the idea that they might delay an enemy until reinforcements could arrive. Castles were usually designed so that a large area around them would be clear of any cover for the enemy. These areas were considered primary target areas where fire could be concentrated. In protecting a castle, horsemen—riders for the baron or king—would regularly patrol in a 4- to 8-mile (6.4 to 12.8-km) radius of the castle, and at times they had to repel small groups of invaders.

Much of the space in the bailey in early castles and the inner ward of later castles was used for stables, blacksmiths, armorers, storehouses, and bunkhouses for this group of castle defenders. The great size of this area, particularly in the early castles, made it difficult to guard against surprise attack. If an additional army arrived to help defend the castle, they also camped within the outer walls or outer ward of the castle.

Often neither side had unlimited manpower to sacrifice in a bloody battle. If a king wanted to overtake more than one castle, he couldn't waste too many men on any single one. A baron didn't have an army of such a large size, so he had to hope that in the event of an attack, his castle would keep him reasonably safe from raiders.

As castle design continued to improve, castles were built to withstand heavier attacks. Square towers were more vulnerable to attack than round ones since missiles would glance off a round tower, but could knock a corner off a square tower.

A trebuchet—or medieval wooden catapult—was often used by those attacking a castle. A trebuchet worked much like a giant slingshot. A missile such as a huge boulder was put in the sling; a winch then wound the beam down on the other end. When the beam was released, the missile was hurled forward. It was very dangerous to be inside the castle when boulders were being flung from outside the walls, because no one could be completely sure where they would land. A trebuchet could also hurl a dead horse or other animal carcass or even a human body into the castle. The attackers hoped that the decaying body would make those within the castle ill as the remains spread disease. The trebuchet was an ideal weapon because it was not heavy and could be moved up and down along the outside of a castle wall.

Another weapon used was the ballista. This was a large crossbow mounted on a stand. The men who handled these machines worked within very close range of the castle and had to be protected from arrows by wooden frames covered over with thick ox hides known as mantlets. These mantlets

Two weapons used in attacking the castle were the catapult and the battering ram.

could be moved along the wall for protection as the machines were moved.

The attacking soldiers usually made their battle machines from timber near the battleground because the machines were too awkward to carry long distances.

The castle defenders might have their own machines on the wall or in the towers. They might also try to sneak out of the castle through a postern or side door, rush the enemy machines, and burn them. The enemy could rebuild the machines, but that took valuable time.

When attacking the curtain of a castle, it was difficult to climb up a ladder with one hand and fight with the other while the soldiers on the castle wall could fight with two hands and could also push the ladder away from the wall. A piece of equipment often built to use at the wall or curtain was a tall wooden tower on wheels that could be pushed up to the curtain. It was called a siege tower. The top of the siege tower was protected with ox hides and men would not be in the open until they reached the curtain itself.

Until the age of gunpowder, one of the most popular ways of attacking a castle, often during an artillery barrage, was to knock a hole in a wall. By using a mantlet for protection, the enemy could reach the base of the wall. Then they could take out stones with a pick or use a battering ram suspended from an overhead beam by ropes.

The first stone castles without protruding towers had little defense against this method. With the development of towers, archers had an improved range of fire to reach those at the base of the wall. Later, the wooden or stone hoards hanging over the curtain had holes in the floors so that stones or boiling liquids could be poured down on those attacking the wall. Castle defenders were even known to melt

Attacking a Castle

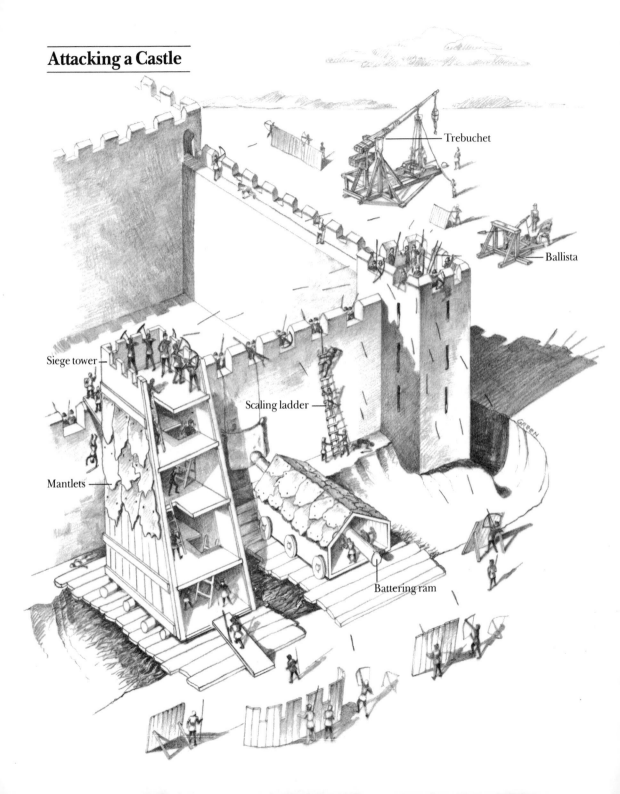

Trebuchet

Ballista

Siege tower

Scaling ladder

Mantlets

Battering ram

down part of lead roofs so they could pour molten lead onto the enemy, although this happened only as a last, desperate resort.

Later castles had what was called a batter at the base of the curtain. The foot of the wall was thicker and would be more difficult to pick through than the rest of the wall. The thick part sloped outward so that stones or missiles dropped from above would shatter and glance off, hitting the enemy.

Building an underground mine was another effective way of attacking castle walls. The enemy would begin a tunnel beyond arrow range and dig to the wall. By removing foundation stones, they would shore up the area with timbers as they worked, making it similar to the inside of a coal mine, until a large chamber was dug. Then they would fill it with material that burns easily, such as straw, brush, or sometimes even pig carcasses. When the material was set on fire, it would burn down the timber supports, causing that part of the wall to collapse and giving the enemy entry into the castle. This was a slow process that required some skill, and would not work on moated castles or those built on rock. The only defense against mines was for those within the castle to burrow into the tunnel and kill the miners or damage the entrance to the mine.

By the early 1300s, design advances had made castles difficult to penetrate. Round towers with arrow slits or loopholes placed along the length of the curtain at bow range defended every section at the foot of the curtain. The sloped batter design of the foot also discouraged using a pick or battering ram. The strong gatehouse made the entrance as mighty as the rest of the castle. There was no one easy way to defeat a well-designed castle. It was truly a center of power.

SIX

CASTLE LIFE

Because castles were built for safety and not for comfort, they were cold, drafty places. Those who lived in castles had little privacy. There were few rooms and many people to house. One possible advantage to this open living was that the presence of so many bodies together helped to warm the rooms!

The living quarters of a castle during the twelfth century centered around the great hall. The great hall was a large open room, which was often a separate building with a huge hearth and a high, expansive ceiling where smoke would escape through a louver or covered opening that served in place of a chimney. Sometimes the great hall was on the first or second floor of the keep, as in most German castles.

The king or baron ate in public in the great hall. This was also where he conducted any business, or affairs of state, or greeted visitors. In the evenings he would be entertained there. Those living in a castle led very active lives and didn't have much time for leisure activities, but in the evenings they

*The great hall of the northern Italian castle,
Castello di Issogne, built in the fifteenth century*

might play chess, checkers, or dice, or be entertained with songs and stories that were accompanied by stringed instruments such as a harp or lute.

The great hall had benches and long trestle tables. For dining, each person was placed according to rank, with the lord and lady seated first in the place of honor. Then guests and knights would be seated. Ladies' maids were sometimes required to eat elsewhere in the castle. Attendants stood until the lord retired for the evening.

Breakfast was a minor meal, usually consisting of bread and ale. The main meal, dinner, came around ten or eleven in the morning. Then in the evening came supper, a smaller meal than dinner. In addition to meat and bread, castle dwellers ate common poultry such as chicken and turkey as well as birds such as gulls, starlings, pigeons, swans, peacocks, herons, and larks. When available, fish, such as herring, was also eaten. Many fruits and vegetables common today were also available, such as onions, peas, cabbage, leeks, apples, and pears. A salad might include garlic, parsley, mint, sage, or fennel with an oil-and-vinegar dressing. Banquet food might feature pig's head, roast pork, fish, venison, pheasant, pies and puddings, along with bread and ale. Wine was usually reserved for the lord and his honored guests.

Everything was eaten with the fingers until the early fourteenth century. Eventually, the king did have silver eating utensils for his meals while others had utensils carved out of wood or animal horn. In addition, stale crusts of bread from the previous day, called trenchers, were sometimes used as plates!

There were usually two kitchens—one for the preparation of the king's food, and one for his men. The well would be located within the castle walls and as close to the kitchens as possible.

An illustration depicting a medieval feast

When they retired at night, the lord and lady had their own bedchamber but the knights slept dormitory style on the floor of the great hall until about the 1300s. By then, there were bedrooms or dormitories for most castle dwellers.

The bed in the lord's chamber was one of the most important pieces of furniture because it might also be used in the daytime as his throne when receiving guests. It was made with a wooden frame and interlaced leather or rope springs, a feather mattress, sheets, quilts, and pillows. Sometimes there was a low bed stored under the king's bed that would be pulled out for honored guests who were staying the night. There were curtains around the king's bed for privacy at night, and these could be rolled up during the day.

A king would often carry his bed with him when he was traveling from castle to castle. He would also take small pieces of furniture, and his tapestries, dishes, and crockery in a wagon train, leaving behind a nearly empty castle.

When a king left his castle, he would order a small group, about twenty cavalrymen, ten archers, and four sentries, to guard the castle. If he had many castles, he might have a constable in charge of each to oversee it in his absence. There might also be a steward who would be sure to prepare the castle for his return, taking special care that there was enough food and places to sleep for any guests who might accompany the king.

In a large castle a lord might have a solar, which was a separate sitting room for his family along with the bedroom. This would be the most comfortable room in the castle with plastered and brightly decorated or painted walls.

There were few chairs in castles. It was considered an honor to be asked to sit in one, although they were not very comfortable. Window seats were popular, and were recessed into the building at right angles to the window. The seat on

*A bedroom in the Palazzo
Davanzati in Florence, Italy*

either side of the window created the effect of a small room. Window seats had the best light for sewing or other close work. Windows near the ground were narrow for security reasons, and most had iron grills and wooden shutters. A few windows in the living quarters might have glass, but this was quite a luxury until the fifteenth century. Most windows were covered with oiled paper and shutters.

The living quarters and the great hall were adorned with colorful tapestries that not only brightened the rooms, but also helped cut down on drafts. Most rooms had their own fireplaces. In the evenings, candles or oil lamps were placed around the walls of each room. All the floors throughout the castle were covered with grasses and sweet-smelling herbs which were swept up and replaced each month. In the great hall, their sweet odor helped hide the smell of dropped food and bones from mealtimes.

Personal belongings such as clothes, documents, and papers were kept in wooden chests similar to cedar chests of today. There were no shelves for storage until later in the Middle Ages.

The bathroom or toilet was referred to as the garderobe. Garderobes were built into the inner and outer curtain. The toilet seat itself was a slab of stone with a round hole in it, and there was a small window or arrow loop in the room for light. The garderobes built into the outer curtain were designed so that the seat extended beyond the face of the wall, allowing waste to fall outside the castle. Garderobes built in the inner wall were over a vertical shaft that led to a cesspit that had to be cleaned out periodically. Clothes were often stored in the garderobes because the odor helped keep the moths away. The word "wardrobe" is reported to have come from this use of the garderobe. Hay was used for toilet paper.

There were many duties in a castle so there had to be plenty of servants—stablehands, tailors, launderers, ladies' maids, bakers, brewers, cooks, candlemakers, and blacksmiths. Armorers took care of the weapons, kept the mail armor clean, and the swords sharp. A keeper of the wardrobe cared for the lord's clothes.

Dogs and cats were allowed to roam the inner ward freely to cut down on rodents. One corner of the inner ward sometimes would be fenced off as a small garden. Hay and food for the animals were usually in hidden storage so it could not easily be found and burned if the castle were under attack.

On special occasions, castle dwellers might hold outdoor activities such as mock battles or tournaments. There were also hunting and falconry in which birds of prey were trained to kill small animals.

Warfare was considered a permanent part of life, so there was always a need to train young noblemen to become knights. From the age of seven, boys in castles were taught the business of war. There was great pressure to measure up to what was expected of a brave knight. At seven, a knight-in-training was removed from the women of the castle and often taken to another castle of a relative or friend to receive such training. It was thought he would learn better from those outside his immediate family.

He would learn horsemanship, the use of a lance, and hand-to-hand combat with two-handed swords and axes. He also had to get accustomed to the weight of armor and its restrictions.

In training he was expected to hunt and participate in tournaments and mock battles. In his early days of training, he would wait on tables, carve meat, and attend to the ladies as a page or servant, for being in service was highly

Knights wore heavy armor to protect themselves.

respected. At the age of fifteen, he became a squire. He was involved in hunting and the care of horses and arms, and waited on knights going into battle or tournaments. Ideally, he also learned how to read, write poetry, and manage his business affairs.

When he became a knight, he was dubbed so with a gentle blow from another knight. Then he would need to show his skill in handling arms and horses. After that, he was considered a knight to be honored and respected.

Knights and horsemen were protected by leather hauberks or tunics until the beginning of the twelfth century when mail armor was used. This armor was made from small overlapping loops of chain and gave solid protection against arrow and lance points, but it didn't prevent the breaking of bones or bad bruising.

Helmets were cone shaped. Early ones had a nose protection that extended down between the eyes. The helmet was often pounded from a single piece of iron.

When, later in the twelfth century, the crossbow was developed, stronger armor was needed, and solid metal armor was worn. A barrel-shaped helmet that rested on the shoulders took some of the weight off the head and replaced the earlier cone-shaped helmet.

A knight also carried a shield for protection which in the early days was quite large. By the thirteenth century, when more armor was worn, such a large shield was cumbersome and unnecessary. A smaller shield was carried that was decorated with symbols and colors that identified the knight. Without this identification, it was difficult to distinguish one knight in his armor from another.

SEVEN

CASTLES IN THE
LATE MIDDLE AGES

By the fourteenth century, castles used cannons for defense, but they were very unreliable. The strength of the gunpowder varied; the cannon could explode if it was packed too tightly. Each cannon was different and required particular tools that worked only when used on that specific type.

Cannons were clumsy to move. Usually a new stand was built in each location and only the tube actually moved from place to place. Cannon balls had to be sized to fit each cannon. Early cannon balls were made of stone. The French were the first to use metal, finding that metal cannon balls traveled faster and were harder. Also, they didn't shatter like stone upon impact.

As cannons were not reliable, battles were still won by longbowmen, knights, and soldiers who did the actual fighting. They used many of the earlier weapons of battle, including objects such as stones, boulders, flaming objects, and carcasses.

It wasn't until about a hundred years later, during the fifteenth century, that the design of the cannon had improved so that they were large and effective enough for soldiers attacking castles. Advancing armies often used cannons to destroy a castle and town walls. The vertical stone walls of a castle could not withstand cannon shot for long.

Many castles used improved, more sophisticated cannons for defense, but the recoil from the cannons shook the masonry loose from the curtain or tower. High towers prevented moving cannons around easily, and the ramparts or sentry walks were too narrow. Cannons mounted inside towers were dangerous not only because of their recoil against the walls but also because the poor ventilation in the tower caused the gunners to choke on gases coming from their own cannons.

The Bastille, a mighty fortress in Paris, started a trend in the 1300s in which some castles were built with the curtain and tower equal in height. This meant that soldiers could rush to any threatened section of the curtain without being slowed by going through tower doors or up tower steps. Soon to follow in France were Pierrefonds Castle, begun in 1392, and Tarascon Castle, in 1400. Both were strong military castles with curtains and towers of the same height.

Elsewhere gunpowder really didn't bring about any major changes in castle design until the early 1500s, when stone walls and towers could not stand up to the improved cannons. Rather than towers, these castles then had bastions built which were equal to the curtain in height and high enough to get a good range on advancing armies. A bastion was a solid round platform that was flat on top so that cannons could be moved at different angles to gain a freer range

of fire. These bastions were built to withstand the recoil of the large guns.

In older castles, the blacksmith who lived there provided weapons for the soldiers. Neither cannons nor cannon balls could be produced by the local blacksmith. More sophisticated skills were required, which were not available locally. This made cannon warfare expensive. Only kings and rulers could afford it and the fortifications that a castle needed to withstand artillery. Sometimes just the sight of cannons was so frightening that no one ever had to fire them.

By the fourteenth century, armies were larger and better trained. Castles couldn't hold out long against ten thousand or more soldiers. The design of castles began to change as military needs changed. Servants no longer worked in exchange for the use of some land, but expected to be paid. A castle owner, therefore, had to be wealthy in order to maintain his castle. The servants' living accommodations had to be more attractive since they would no longer work under the old cramped conditions. There had to be halls for visitors and barracks for soldiers.

The soldiers were called professionals or mercenaries because they hired themselves out to a ruler and fought for him because they were paid well, not because they felt an allegiance to him. Because soldiers were professional and trained in the business of fighting, the owner of the castle didn't worry so much about defense. But he also didn't know the soldiers as well, so he wanted to separate them from his own family by providing them with barracks.

Pierrefonds Castle

By the fifteenth and sixteenth centuries, the few castles that were being built became more like country homes, although they may have kept some early defense features such as a moat for appearance's sake. The style of building changed and included higher-pitched roofs and more ornamental decoration. Tower castles had towers that were more decorative and more flamboyant than they were useful, including those of Dunrobin Castle and Thirlestane Castle in Scotland. Castles built during this time were spacious and had larger windows and therefore better lighting.

The way people lived became more formal, as there was less time and energy spent on fighting. Although knights were still honored in society, knighthood skills were no longer taught. Rules were developed that applied to castle life, hunting, and fighting. More money was spent on clothes which, in turn, became more fashionable. Social functions such as weddings, parties, and royal banquets became elaborate and expensive. Life in general became much easier.

Although some still had a military purpose, many of the older castles were remodeled during the fourteenth century. More living space and personal comforts were added, and castles began to resemble huge country estates or fortified manor homes. These castles with their wealth and power could influence people and create political connections. Two castles that were remodeled during this time were Kenilworth Castle and Windsor Castle in England.

The castles built during the fourteenth, fifteenth, and sixteenth centuries were either quadrilateral castles or tower houses. The quadrilateral plan allowed for spacious, open courts. Quadrilateral castles covered large rectangular areas and had round towers at the corners, square towers in the middle, and usually two gatehouses. Some of these were built

*Chambord Castle, in France, is
an ornately decorated castle.*

with large gun loops in place of arrow slits. The gun loops looked like huge keyholes.

Bodiam Castle in England was one of the first castles in Europe to have big gun loops. Begun in 1385, Bodiam was a quadrilateral castle and is one of the few moated castles remaining today. Although impressive, Bodiam Castle wasn't as strong as it looked. It was not a concentric castle. There was only one line of curtain and the ramparts or sentry walks did not connect with each other. To get from one tower to another, a soldier had to go down into the courtyard and up again. Since the soldiers were professionals, the lord did not want them in the family rooms in the towers. So to maintain family privacy, there was no quick passage from rampart to rampart. Bodiam was attacked in 1483 and surrendered immediately.

The tower houses reflected the reintroduction of the earlier keep design. They were very tall and impressive-looking, but were still more palatial homes than defensive castles. Nunney Castle in England was a tower house built in the late fourteenth century. Tower houses were constructed in many countries such as Czechoslovakia, France, Spain, and Scotland. Karlstejn in Czechoslovakia, Tattershall in England, and Pierrefonds in France were all tower houses of striking height.

However, not all of the tower castles only *looked* impressive. Peñafiel Castle in Spain had a tall keep rising above an elaborate curtain wall and was built with the emphasis on

Bodiam Castle in
Sussex, England

(72)

defense. Another castle, in Fuensaldaña, Spain, had a high tower keep but was never finished or occupied. Both of these were built in the fifteenth century. Those in Scotland also emphasized defense. Craigievar Castle, finished in 1626, had the older narrow windows and strong entrances, whereas most tower houses in other countries had larger, fashionable windows for improved lighting.

It was difficult to place furniture in round tower rooms, and since, in most countries, comfort and appearance were now more important than defense, square towers were built in the few castles that were still being constructed, with bricks more often used than stone in the castle's construction. Sometimes colored glass was placed in the windows, but it was very expensive.

EIGHT

THE DECLINE
OF THE CASTLE

The improvement of the cannon for use in aggressive warfare marked the decline of the castle era. Castles built during the fourteenth, fifteenth, and sixteenth centuries were admired as objects of remarkable beauty, but were no longer feared. Perhaps this also led indirectly to their eventual decline.

By the 1500s, the strength of regional lords had lessened, and centralized governments had taken their place. Kings and lords fought less among themselves than they had in feudal societies. Serfs who had worked for a baron no longer wanted to stay in the local village. The cities were more attractive to them, and there they could earn better wages.

By the sixteenth century, most private castles were used as huge country homes. In countries where a ruler or king reigned peacefully, castles were no longer built because strongholds were not necessary. The few castles that were built were constructed for the sake of appearance. Conve-

Above: *Llanstephan Castle in Wales is a decaying thirteenth century castle.* Right: *today, this castle in the Loire Valley, France, is a hotel.*

nience and luxury were important; defense was not. People preferred to rely on the king's protection.

A large number of castles fell into ruin because they were not cared for. Others had modifications or luxurious ornaments added, and weren't castles at all.

In Great Britain, after the civil war in 1642, and in France, many castles were either supplied with soldiers or were ruined. It was expensive to keep men in them, so most were torn down or damaged so that they would not become a center of resistance to the government. Often a hole was created in the curtain wall and one wall of the keep destroyed, which left the castle useless for defensive purposes. Then local neighbors were encouraged to plunder the castle, taking what building materials were available. They often took the timbers of rafters and the lead from the roof and left the castle open to the damp weather. Walls were then split by frost as joints in the stonework loosened. Ivy roots pushed them further apart and the dampness rotted the plaster until there was little left but the crumbling ruins seen today.

Some castles were still used in times of trouble such as a civil war, but more became peaceful refuges rather than powerful centers of warfare. Some were turned into museums or centers of government administration. Some were used as prisons and places of execution. A few

The Castle of Chillon,
in the Lake Geneva
region of Switzerland,
has become a museum.

remained as armed military installations and observation posts into the nineteenth and twentieth centuries.

However, the majority of castles that have survived to the present day serve as tourist attractions and private residences. Some are visited as ruins, but many have been restored for visitors. Often they also contain a museum of medieval weapons, armor, clothes, and furniture. By opening these castles to the public, money is brought in to help pay for their upkeep. By preserving castles and studying them, it is possible to continue learning about castles and their significance in history.

NINE

LEGENDS AND
GHOST STORIES

Castles are linked with a period in history that has been the setting for many adventure and fantasy stories. Few written records have survived from the Middle Ages, but it has become a time we connect with magic, sorcery, romanticism, and adventure. There are many legends and stories associated with the castles themselves. If castle walls could talk, they would have stories to tell us. They could tell of the many families who had lived there, who had died there, and both the good and evil deeds that were carried out within them. As in all stories told over and over, it is difficult to separate fact from fiction. Here are just a few stories and legends about some castles. You can decide for yourself what to believe.

Harlech Castle, Wales

The earliest written record of this story was around A.D. 1225. Bendigeidfran, the King of Britain and a giant of a man, sat on the rocks of Harlech watching the sea, as he often did. While there, he saw thirteen ships approaching his castle. He sent men out in his own ships to see what business these strangers had. The first ship approached with an upturned shield, a sign of peace. Matholwch, the King of Ireland, embarked on land and spoke to Bendigeidfran, making his wishes known. He wanted to marry the king's sister, Branwen, who was a fair and beautiful maiden.

Bendigeidfran agreed to Matholwch's request to marry Branwen. But when Branwen's other brother, the jealous and quarrelsome Efinisien, learned of the proposed marriage, he was so angry that to spite the Irish king he maimed Matholwch's horses while they were in the Harlech stables. Matholwch was furious when he found out, and King Bendigeidfran had to offer many gifts to soothe the Irish king. Matholwch accepted the gifts and finally set out with his new bride for Ireland.

Things went well for the first two years, but the story of the slain horses reached the Irish people. They became angry and took out their anger on Branwen, banishing her to the kitchen.

Desperately, Branwen prayed that her brother, King Bendigeidfran, would come to her rescue. Her only friend was a little sparrow who watched her knead dough every day at her worktable. An idea came to her. She would try to teach him her language and then send him to Wales as a messenger.

The sparrow carried a message under his wing to the king. King Bendigeidfran wanted to hurry to his sister's rescue. Rather than wait for boats to be readied for the trip, being a giant, he stretched his body out across the sea. His warriors then marched over him to Ireland.

A battle raged and Bendigeidfran rescued his sister. But the battle was long and hard, and the Welsh had many more casualties than the Irish. Efinisien, who was fighting for his king, wondered why this was so and discovered the Irish soldiers' secret. They had a magic cauldron into which they put the dead, and the dead emerged alive.

Efinisien, who was not wholly bad, threw himself into the cauldron and stretched out across it, splitting it apart so that it could not be used. He perished but, in so doing, saved his brother's men. King Bendigeidfran and the few men he had remaining returned with Branwen to Anglesey, an island off the coast of Wales.

Branwen was very upset and suffered great anguish that the brave of two nations had died for her. Finally, she died of a broken heart and was laid to rest on the banks of a river in a place still called Bedd Branwen, or "Branwen's Grave."

Edinburgh Castle, Scotland

At one time in history, the body of the mother of Mary, Queen of Scots lay in a coffin in a room on the upper floor of Edinburgh Castle. The body was there for more than eight months before finally being buried. Members of families who live in the castle and earn their living working there say they sometimes feel a cold presence enter a room and hear a rustle of skirts, but they see nothing. However, some of the elders of these families, now deceased, claimed to have seen this ghost at various times. Once she was at a woman's bedside and another time she walked across the stone courtyard on a dark evening.

Stirling Castle, Scotland

John Damian, a local Scotsman, once told the king that he was going to fly to Turkey from the wall of Stirling Castle.

He then prepared to fly by constructing some wings and adding chicken feathers to them. The day of his departure arrived, and he jumped from the wall, flapping his wings with all his might. Unfortunately, he flew more vertically than horizontally, landing with a broken back on the ground.

He apologized to the king, and told him that he should have known better than to use chicken feathers, because chickens don't fly!

Another story about Stirling Castle tells about a ghost that appears every fifty years. It is called the Green Lady and is thought to be the ghost of Margaret Drummond, who was the mistress of King James IV. Margaret Drummond was one of three sisters who were all poisoned one evening at an outing. It seems that someone who was jealous of her position with the king poisoned both her and her sisters. Like clockwork, every fifty years, the Green Lady has reappeared as if to remind all of the injustice that was done to her.

Dunrobin Castle, Scotland

The ghost of Margaret, the daughter of the fourteenth Earl of Sutherland, still haunts Dunrobin Castle. She fell in love with Jamie Gunn, the son of a servant to the Earl, and her father, of course, disapproved, feeling that Jamie Gunn was not worthy of her. The two met secretly, however, and their love grew. Jamie Gunn carved their initials in a rock that still marks a place by a cave in Dunrobin Glen.

The Earl, wishing to stop their romance, ordered Margaret not to see Jamie. Margaret tried to run away, but the Earl's steward, who had been keeping watch, thwarted her efforts. The Earl then locked her away in a small dark attic room with a guard posted at the foot of the stairs twenty-four hours a day.

Margaret tried to keep up her spirits, but her sobs and wails could be heard throughout the castle at night. Her maid, Morag, desperately wanted to help her mistress, for Margaret was slowly pining away of a broken heart. Unable to stand it any longer, Morag decided to help Margaret try to escape. Morag would deliver a long rope to Margaret hidden under her skirt at mealtime, and Margaret would climb down the rope to Jamie, who would be waiting with two horses.

The night for the planned escape arrived, but the steward was again keeping watch and discovered that something was wrong. Margaret was on the ledge outside her window, preparing to lower herself down the rope, when her father burst through the door.

"Stop! Never shall you marry that rascal!" he cried.

Margaret, startled by his entry, lost her grip and fell to her death, crying, "Then I shall marry no one."

Jamie went to her in anguish and realized it was too late. She was dead, and he had to get away.

He looked at the Earl who was still at the window, shocked by what had happened, and shouted, "May she haunt you evermore!"

Today those who work in the castle still hear mournful sobs coming from the small dark attic room.

Tower of London, England

Anne Boleyn, the second wife of King Henry VIII, was beheaded at the Tower of London in the 1500s. Her ghost has been seen a number of times since then, but probably never more explicitly than in the 1800s in the Chapel of the

White Tower. There was a light burning in the locked chapel late one night, and the Captain of the Guard went to investigate. He climbed a ladder to look into one of the windows.

What he saw almost knocked him from his perch. Inside, there was a procession of knights and ladies dressed in ancient clothing. The group repeatedly walked back and forth through the chapel led by a woman whom the guard took to be Anne Boleyn from the many portraits he had seen of her. Eventually, after a number of stately trips up and down the floor of the chapel, the procession and the light disappeared into the air.

Glamis Castle, Scotland

Glamis Castle lies in the heart of what is known as the fairy region of Scotland. The castle is said to be the oldest continually inhabited castle in the country. But the original and oldest part of the castle was to be built on a hill nearby that was also the place where fairies lived. During the day workers would begin the building; by night, the fairies would scatter the stones so that their work was always in vain. Finally, the disgruntled builder moved his stones to Glamis's present location. But the central part of the castle, which is the oldest part, still has many reports of hauntings, strange sounds and sights appearing in the early morning predawn hours, those hours when fairies are supposed to be most active.

Fyvie Castle, Scotland

Fyvie Castle has a secret room with no access. There have been many attempts to secure entrance into this room in the hope of finding reputed treasure. However, there is a curse that goes with any attempt to gain admittance: that the owner will die and his wife will be blinded for life. This curse has not stopped some from tempting fate. A General Gordon once attempted to open the room, and died shortly after his attempt. His wife soon became blind.

Another man, Sir Maurice Duff-Gordon, tried to open the room. While workmen were attempting to find a passageway, he slipped and fell in the drawing room and broke his leg. Fearful of further repercussion, he halted the work, but not soon enough, as his wife contracted an eye irritation that remained with her for the rest of her life.

GLOSSARY

arrow slit: Long, narrow vertical opening in the castle wall from which arrows could be shot at the enemy.

bailey: The outer wall of an early castle and the space enclosed within that section, usually oval or rectangular in shape.

ballista: Medieval weapon that was similar to a large crossbow mounted on a stand.

barbican: An outer tower of the castle that defended the approaches to the gatehouse or bridge.

bastion: A solid platform that replaced the tower in later castles. Its top was flat with no crenellations so that cannons placed there could be shot freely in any direction.

batter: The bottom or foot of the outside wall or curtain of a castle that was thicker and sloped outward.

battering ram: A heavy wooden beam used to batter walls.

concentric castle: A castle with two complete sets of walls, one within the other.

crenellated: The toothed appearance of the top of a castle wall or curtain. The gaps in the wall are called crenels.

curtain: The wall around the castle usually connected by towers.

drawbridge: A bridge across a wet or dry moat that could be raised to prevent access into the castle.

feudal system: An economic and political system in which two free men, usually a vassal and his lord, enter a contract where the vassal generally performs military or knight service in exchange for his maintenance. This was usually provided by means of a grant of land, known as a fief.

fief: A unit of land held in exchange for the performance of military service.

garrison: Soldiers stationed in a castle.

gatehouse: Entryway into castle. Usually two towers built with the gate recessed between them. Rooms were built in the archway above the gate and in towers.

gun loop: Keyhole-shaped arrow slit built in later castles that was round at the bottom and large enough for a cannon.

hauberk: A tunic or loose-fitting garment made of leather or chain mail and worn for protection.

hoard: A covered wooden projection that was built on the outside of a castle wall or curtain to allow soldiers to defend the castle from those directly below. These were later built of stone.

keep: The main tower or building of a castle.

King Edward I: King of England A.D. 1272–1307.

louver: A covered hole in the ceiling that kept out rain and let smoke out, serving as a chimney.

mail armor: Flexible armor made of small overlapping metal rings or loops of chain.

mantlet: A protective wooden frame covered with ox hides.

mark: Former English unit of money equal to thirteen shillings and four pence.

merlons: The rising part of a crenellated or toothed wall.

mew: Area where king's or ruler's hunting birds were kept in cages.

moat: A wide, deep ditch, usually filled with water, that surrounded a castle or medieval town as a line of defense.

motte: Raised mound of earth upon which a wooden tower was constructed.

motte-and-bailey castle: An early wooden castle with motte or mound on which a wooden tower was built surrounded by an oval or rectangular bailey on a lower level of land with a gate at the farthest point from the motte.

murder holes: Openings in floors of rooms above the passageway in a gatehouse where hot liquids and rocks could be thrown down on attackers.

palisade: A wooden fence, 10 to 12 feet (3.5 to 4 m) high, surrounding the top of the motte.

portcullis: A heavy wooden grating covered with iron and suspended on chains that could be dropped quickly from above the gatehouse or any doorway.

postern: A small rear or side door or gate in a castle.

quadrilateral castle: A fourteenth or fifteenth century castle with a rectangular area enclosed by a stone wall with round towers at the corners, square flanking towers in the middle, and two gatehouses. A forerunner of the later Tudor houses.

sentry walk: A platform or walkway around the inside top of a castle curtain used by guards, lookouts, and soldiers in defending a castle.

siege tower: A tall wooden tower on wheels covered with ox hide and used when attacking a castle curtain.

shell keep: A stone wall that replaced the wooden wall on top of the motte.

solar: A private sitting room for the royal family, usually adjoining the lord's bedroom on the second floor in later castles.

tower: A round, square, or six-sided structure built into the castle wall, at least one story higher than the wall and containing various rooms.

trebuchet: A medieval catapult for throwing rocks and other objects.

ward: The courtyard of a castle.

winch: A mechanism that lifts or pulls by turning a crank and coiling a rope or cable around a drum.

FURTHER READING

Anderson, William. *Castles of Europe from Charlemagne to the Renaissance.* New York: Random House, 1970.

Brown, R. Allen. *The Architecture of Castles: A Visual Guide.* New York: Facts on File Publication, 1984.

Burke, John. *Life in the Castle in Medieval England.* Totowa, New Jersey: Rowman & Littlefield, 1978.

Duggan, Alfred. *The Castle Book.* New York: Pantheon, 1961.

Gies, Joseph & Frances. *Life in a Medieval Castle.* New York: Harper & Row, 1974.

Johnson, Paul. *The National Trust Book of British Castles.* New York: G. P. Putnam & Sons, 1978.

Macaulay, David. *Castle.* Boston: Houghton Mifflin, 1977.

Oman, Charles. *Castles.* New York: Doubleday, 1926.

Sancha, Sheila. *The Castle Story.* New York: Crowell, 1979.

Thomas, Roger. *Castles in Wales.* Cardiff, Wales: Wales Tourist Board, 1982.

Vaughan, Jenny. *Castles.* New York: Franklin Watts, 1984.

INDEX